Carpet Cleaning: End Money Worries Business Book Secrets to Starting, Financing, Marketing and Making Massive Money Right Now!

by

Brian Mahoney

Get Our Video Training Program at:

(Zero Cost Internet Marketing complete 142 video series)

http://goo.gl/gQnSo4

Massive Money for Real Estate Investing

http://www.BrianSMahoney.com

ABOUT THE AUTHOR

Brian Mahoney is the author of over 100 business start-up guides, real estate investing programs and Christian literature. He started his company MahoneyProducts in 1992.

He served in the US Army and worked over a decade for the US Postal Service. An active real estate investor, he has also served as a minister for the Churches of Christ in Virginia and Michigan.

He has degree's in Business Administration and Applied Science & Computer Programming.

His books and video training programs have helped thousands of people all over the world start there own successful business.

http://www.briansmahoney.com/

DEDICATION

This book is dedicated to my son's
Christian and Matthew.
A blessing from God and the joy of my life.

Table of Contents

Chapter 1 Business Overview

Chapter 2 A Step by Step Plan

Chapter 3 Business Plan

Chapter 4 Free Money to Get Started

Chapter 5 SBA Loans

Chapter 6 Micro Loans

Chapter 7 Legal Structure

Chapter 8 Business Name

Chapter 9 Business Tax Advantages

Chapter 10 How to Hire Employees

Chapter 11 Million Dollar Wholesale Rolodex

Chapter 12 Zero Cost Marketing

Chapter 13 Bonus Material: Motivation

Chapter 14 Bonus Material: Credit Repair

ACKNOWLEDGMENTS

I WOULD LIKE TO ACKNOWLEDGE ALL THE HARD WORK OF THE MEN AND WOMEN OF THE UNITED STATES MILITARY, WHO RISK THEIR LIVES ON A DAILY BASIS, TO MAKE THE WORLD A SAFER PLACE.

Disclaimer

This book was written as a guide to starting a business. As with any other high yielding action, starting a business has a certain degree of risk. This book is not meant to take the place of accounting, legal, financial or other professional advice. If advice is needed in any of these fields, you are advised to seek the services of a professional.

While the author has attempted to make the information in this book as accurate as possible, no guarantee is given as to the accuracy or currency of any individual item. Laws and procedures related to business are constantly changing.

Therefore, in no event shall Brian Mahoney, the author of this book be liable for any special, indirect, or consequential damages or any damages whatsoever in connection with the use of the information herein provided.

Business Overview

Start-up Cost: $2,000-$3,000 leasing equipment, $4,000-$10,000 buying equipment.
Potential Earnings: $35,000-$50,000

Typical Fees: $20 per square foot first; $40 or more each additional room.

Advertising:

Coupon books, Zero Cost Online Marketing, Internet Marketing, Business Cards, Classified Ads, Yellow Pages, Online Yellow Pages, Website, Referrals, Direct Mail Postcards, Business Groups

Qualifications:

Manual labor ready, Organizational skills, strong marketing ability

Equipment Needed:

Carpet Cleaning machine, chemical cleaners, van or truck

Home Business Potential: Yes

Staff Required: No

Hidden Costs:

Insurance & licensing; Travel Expenses

Carpet Cleaning

Carpet cleaning, for appearance, and the removal of stains, dirt, and allergens is done through several methods. Clean carpets are recognized by manufacturers as being more visually pleasing, potentially longer-lasting, and probably healthier than poorly maintained carpets.

Hot Water Extraction

Although there is an actual steam cleaning industrial process, in the context of carpet cleaning, "steam cleaning" is, in fact, hot water extraction cleaning. The hot water extraction cleaning method uses equipment that sprays heated water, sometimes with added cleaning chemicals, on the carpet. Simultaneously, the water is vacuumed up, along with any dislodged and dissolved dirt. Many carpet manufacturers recommend professional hot water extraction as the most effective carpet cleaning methodActual steam could damage man-made carpet fibers or shrink natural fibers such as wool.

Hot water extraction equipment may be a portable unit that plugs into an electrical outlet, or a truck mount carpet cleaner requiring long hoses from the truck or trailer. Truck mounted equipment may be used where electricity is unavailable (e.g. if electrical service was terminated). Truck mount carpet cleaning may be unsuited to premises distant from a driveway or road, and hoses may need to pass through windows to reach upper floors of a building.

Hoses needed for truck mount and professional portable carpet cleaning may present an inconvenience or tripping hazard to users of hallways, and pets or children can escape through doors that must be left ajar for hoses. Heated or air conditioned air will also escape from buildings when doors are left open for hoses, potentially creating a significant waste of energy. Truck mounted carpet cleaning equipment minimizes noise in the room being cleaned, but truck mounted carpet cleaning equipment may cause noise and air pollution offensive to neighbors, and may violate anti-idling bylaws in some jurisdictions. However, truck-mounted cleaning is much faster than portable equipment, and extra heat and power can give faster drying times.

A Rental carpet cleaning machine.

A common process of hot water extraction begins with preconditioning. Alkaline agents such as ammonia solution for synthetic carpets, or acidic solution (such as vinegar solution) for woolen carpets, are sprayed into the carpet, then agitated with a grooming brush or an automatic scrubbing machine. Next, a pressurized manual or automatic cleaning tool (such as a wand) passes over the surface to rinse out all pre-conditioner, residue, and particulates. If an alkaline detergent is used on a woolen fibre, use of an acetic acid solution will restore neutral fiber pH. The acid rinse thus neutralizes the alkaline residues, and can contribute to softening cleaned fabrics.

Extraction is, by far, the most important step in the hot water extraction process. Since the hot-water extraction method uses much more water than other methods like bonnet or shampoo cleaning, proper extraction and air flow are critical to avoid drying issues. Drying time may also be decreased by extra use of fans, air conditioning, and/or outdoor ventilation.

Older surfaces, such as double jute-backed carpets and loose rugs with natural foundation yarns, could shrink after a wet treatment, leading to suppositions that wet-cleaning could also remove wrinkles. However, this notion is antiquated and this method could also occasionally tear seams or uproot strips. Newer carpets, such as with synthetic backing and foundation yarns, do not shrink, and they smooth easily; in such carpets, wrinkles indicate an underlying problem, such as adhesive, that may need a certified carpet inspector to determine.

Wet-cleaning systems naturally require drying time, which may lead to concerns about very slow drying, the risk of discoloration returning during drying, and odors, bacteria, fungi, molds, and mildews. Carpet cleaning specialists try to find a balance between rapid drying (attributable to lower flow rate through the cleaning jets of a spray system) and the need to remove the most soil (attributable to higher flow rate).

Pretreatments similar to those in dry-cleaning and "very low moisture" systems are employed, but require a longer dwell time of 15 to 20 minutes, because of lower amounts of carpet agitation. Ideal pretreatments should rinse easily and leave dry, powdery, or crystalline residue that can be flushed without contributing to re-soiling.

Dry-cleaning

Many dry carpet-cleaning systems rely on specialized machines. These systems are mostly "very low moisture" (VLM) systems, relying on dry compounds complemented by application cleaning solutions, and are growing significantly in market share due in part to their very rapid drying time, a significant factor for 24-hour commercial installations. Dry-cleaning and "very low moisture" systems are also often faster and less labor-intensive than wet-extraction systems.

Heavily soiled areas require the application of manual spotting, pretreatments, preconditioners, and/or "traffic-lane cleaners", (commonly sprayed onto carpet prior to the primary use of the dry-cleaning system) which are detergents or emulsifiers which break the binding of different soils to carpet fibers over a short period of time. For example, one chemical may dissolve the greasy films that bind soils to the carpet, and thus prevent effective soil removal through vacuuming. The solution may add a solvent like d-limonene, petroleum byproducts, glycol ethers, or butyl agents.

The amount of time the pretreatment dwells in the carpet should be less than 15 minutes, due to the thorough carpet brushing common to these "very low moisture" systems, which provides added agitation to ensure the pretreatment works fully through the carpet. The benefit of dry carpet cleaning, over wet solutions, is that dry chemical compounds don't attract dirt, like dried shampoo. While dry carpet cleaning is more expensive and more time consuming to clean than Bonnet or extraction, dry cleaning formulas put less stress on the carpets themselves. Dry compound

A 98% biodegradable or others, slightly moist absorbent cleaning compound may be spread evenly over carpet and brushed or scrubbed in. For small areas, a household hand brush can work such a compound into carpet pile; working like "tiny sponges", the attracted cleaning solution dissolve dirt, dirt and grime is attracted/absorbed to the compound, after a short drying time (the cleaning solution which is attracted to the compound must evaporate), it will be removed with a vacuum cleaner, the drier the better, leaving carpet immediately clean and dry. But it's very difficult to remove all residues, the residues can cause allergies and biological compounds may cause discolourations on carpets. For commercial applications, a specially designed cylindrical counter-rotating brushing system is used, without a vacuum cleaner. Machine scrubbing is more typical, in that hand scrubbing generally cleans only the top third of carpet.

Encapsulation

In the 1990s, new polymers began literally encapsulating (crystallizing) soil particles into dry residues on contact. In the conventional cleaning process surfactant molecules attach themselves to oily soil particles, suspending them (emulsification) so that they can be easily rinsed away. Surfactant (detergent) molecules and emulsified soils which escape being rinsed away, remain in the fibre and continue to attract soiling, causing the condition of the carpet to degenerate; often re-soiling faster than before it was subjected to the cleaning process. Encapsulators are speciality detergent polymers which become part of the detergent system. As drying occurs (20-30 min. drytime), after cleaning, these encapsulators bind the detergent molecules and residual soils in a brittle, crystalline structure. Detergent and soil particles can no longer attract other soils and are easily removed by dry vacuuming. In addition to binding the detergent and soil residues the encapsulation chemistry coats the clean fibre with the same brittle film. This reduces the fibre's affinity for oily and particulate soils. As this brittle film"breaks away" and more soil is removed, the appearance of the fibre improves as opposed to soiling more rapidly. Products which also employ fluorochemical technology, display dramatically extended anti re-soiling time periods. Cleaning solution is applied by rotary machine, brush applicator, or compression sprayer.

Dry residue is vacuumable immediately (20-30 min. drytime), either separately or from a built-in unit of the cleaning-system machine. According to ICS Cleaning Specialist, evidence suggests encapsulation improves carpet appearance, compared to other systems; and it is favorable in terms of high-traffic needs, operator training, equipment expense, and lack of wet residue. Encapsulation carpet cleaning also keeps carpets cleaner for longer periods of time compared to other methods. Encapsulation also avoids the drying time of carpet shampoos, making the carpet immediately available for use. The use of encapsulation to create a crystalline residue that can be immediately (20-30 min. drytime) vacuumed (as opposed to the residue of wet cleaning systems, which generally requires an additional day before vacuuming) is a newer technology that has recently become an accepted method for commercial and residential deep cleaning.

Bonnet

After club soda mixed with cleaning product, other products are also possible, is deposited onto the surface as mist, a round buffer or "bonnet" scrubs the mixture with rotating motion. This industry machine resembles a floor buffer, with an absorbent spin or oscillating pad that attracts soil and is rinsed or replaced repeatedly. The bonnet method is not strictly dry-cleaning and involves significant drying time.

To reduce pile distortion, the absorbent bonnet should be kept well-lubricated with cleaning solution. Its not recommended to dunk the bonnet in a bucket of cleaning solution and then wring it out with a mop-bucket wringer, then the bonnet is to wet. Its very important to change or turn the bonnet early, Bonnets can become filled with soil in just a couple hundred square feet. And once loaded with soil, the bonnet will not hold any more; instead, it simply moves the soil from one area to another. The overly wet bonnet also deposits residues that attract soils when they are dry, creating the need to clean more often. Its recommended for robust and not for high floor carpet, it swirls the floor. It distorts pile and grinds dirt deeper in carpet fiber also it has an abrasive effect. When there is a large amount of foreign material in the carpet, extraction with a wet process may be needed. Normally, the spin-bonnet method may not be as capable of sanitizing carpet fibers due to the lack of hot water, for this a spezial thermo machine is needed, here the buffing machine is equipped with a heating, to heat up the bonnet, but a post-cleaning application of an antimicrobial agent is used to make up for this. Compared to steam cleaning, the small amounts of water required with spin-bonnet carpet cleaning favor water-conservation considerations. It only cleans the top of the carpet 1/8 inch but its very fast for wide areas.

But bonnet cleaning is not the best mechanism for completely removing the chemical that is pre-sprayed onto a carpet. Its recommended that only surfactant free or encapsulating products are used. On the other hand, the re-soiling is great.

Shampoo

Wet shampoo cleaning with rotary machines, followed by thorough wet vacuuming, was widespread until about the 1970s, but industry perception of shampoo cleaning changed with the advent of encapsulation. Hot-water extraction, also regarded as preferable, had not been introduced either. Wet shampoos were once formulated from coconut oil soaps; wet shampoo residues can be foamy or sticky, and steam cleaning often reveals dirt unextracted by shampoos. Since no rinse is performed, the powerful residue can continue to collect dirt after cleaning, leading to the misconception that carpet cleaning can lead to the carpet getting "dirtier faster" after the cleaning. The best method is to combine shampoo and extraction, first shampoo with a spin brush to loosen the dirt and the pile, then extraction the carpet. But this needs time and double rinsed is necessary and the drying time is up to 24 hours.

When wet-shampoo chemistry standards converted from coconut oil soaps to synthetic detergents as a base, the shampoos dried to a powder, and loosened dirt would attach to the powder components, requiring vacuuming by the consumer the day after cleaning.

Dry foam carpet cleaning

Dry foam cleaning involves applying cleaning foam and immediately vacuuming the foam. It is not a completely dry method since the foam is 90% air and 10% liquid. A dry foam machine consists of a pressure tank in which a solution of water and shampoo is added. This method is used for water sensitive carpets, needle felt, and other carpet types whose construction inhibits sufficient water extraction.

Vacuum wash

Vacuum washing employs a washhead that sprays water without detergent and immediately removes it by suction, creating a swirl of water. This ensures high cleaning performance, extracting the dirt from the carpet to a depth of half inch. By immediately reabsorbing the wash water, the drying time greatly shortened. This method is suitable for intermediate and basic cleaning. Because it does not require cleaning products, it leaves no detergent residue.

Vacuum washing has long been in use in Europe, mostly in larger train and bus companies, schools, and historic preservation. The system works on all surfaces which are water resistant (carpet, upholstered furniture, wooden floors, stone, plastics). A great advantage is that this system works without brushes or pads so there is no abrasion on pile.

Household processes

Other household carpet-cleaning processes are much older than industry standardization, and have varying degrees of effectiveness as supplements to the more thorough cleaning methods accepted in the industry.

Vacuum

Vacuum cleaners use air pumps to create partial vacuums to suck up dust and dirt, usually from floors and carpets. Filtering systems or cyclones collect dirt for later disposal. Modern carpet cleaning equipment use rotary vacuum heads and spray jets to deep clean the carpet through hundreds of multi-directional cleaning passes. Some add steam and agitation. Models include upright (dirty-air and clean-air), canister and backpack, wet-dry and pneumatic, and other varieties. Robotic vacuum cleaners have recently become available.

Stain removal

Tea leaves and cut grass were formerly common for floor cleaning, to collect dust from carpets, albeit with risks of stains. Ink was removed with lemon or with oxalic acid and hartshorn; oil with white bread or with pipe clay; grease fats with turpentine; ox gall and naphtha were also general cleaners. Ammonia and chloroform were recommended for acid discoloration. Benzine and alum were suggested for removing insects; diatomaceous earth and material similar to cat litter are still common for removing infestations. Candle wax is removed by placing a towel over the affected carpet area and applying steam from a clothes iron until the wax absorbs into the towel. Some traditional methods of stain removal remain successful and ecological. Caution should be addressed when treating natural fibers such as wool.

The longer the stain material remains in the carpet, the higher the chance of permanent color change, even if all the original stain material is removed. At times pets urinate on the carpet and this results in a bad odor especially when it is hot and humid.The carpet or rug is usually taken outside and immersed in water to remove such stains. Immediately blotting (not rubbing) the stain material as soon as possible will help reduce the chances of permanent color change.

Artificial food coloring stains are generally considered permanent stains. These may be removed by professional cleaners or deep cleaning rental machines with heat-transfer stain-reducing chemicals, but carry risks of burning the carpet. Stain removal products can be combined with anti-allergen treatments to kill house dust mites.

Other

Carpet rods, rattan rugbeaters, and carpet-beating machines for beating out dust, and also brooms, brushes, dustpans, and shaking and hanging were all carpet-cleaning methods of the 19th century; brooms particularly carry risks of wear. Steam cleaning increases the lifespan of your carpet.

Commercial Cleaning

Commercial cleaning is a broad term predominantly used by cleaning companies who earn an income by being contracted by individuals, businesses, or corporations to carry out cleaning jobs in a variety of premises. Cleaning companies can be found in virtually every town and city in the world, with a higher concentration in affluent regions. Typically these companies market their services via a professional sales force, advertising, word of mouth, or websites.

Commercial cleaning may include:

Shops

High-rises

Function Centers

Data Centers

Restaurants

Offices

Showrooms

Warehouses

Factories

Schools

Medical facilities

Government facilities

Airports

Cleaning techniques and equipment

Commercial office cleaning companies use a wide variety of cleaning methods, chemicals, and equipment to facilitate and expedite the cleaning process. The scope of work may include all internal, general and routine cleaning - including floors, tiles, partition walls, internal walls, suspended ceilings, lighting, furniture and cleaning, window cleaning, deep cleans of sanitary conveniences and washing facilities, kitchens and dining areas, consumables and feminine hygiene facilities as well as cleaning of telephones, IT, and other periodic cleaning as required. Carpet cleaning though, even with regular vacuuming, needs hot water extraction applied every 18 to 24 months. External cleaning, litter picking, and removal of graffiti may also be incorporated.

The two global cleaning industry associations, the British Institute of Cleaning Science (BICSc) and the International Sanitary Supply Association (ISSA), both publish standards for managers and operatives engaged in cleaning activities.

Workers

The commercial cleaning industry is extremely competitive and employees tend to be at the lower end of the pay scale. However, unionized workers may earn higher wages. Many commercial cleaning companies provide on-the-job training for all new employees due to the nonexistence of tertiary based courses for the cleaning industry. A trend in the cleaning industry is the elimination of the usage of more hazardous chemicals such as drain cleaners due to liability and environmental concerns. Individuals employed in commercial cleaning typically hold the job title of janitor, custodian, or day porter.

In Australia, the US, and Europe, commercial cleaning companies are encouraged to screen all employees for evidence of a criminal background. In some countries, such as the United Kingdom, cleaners working in schools, children's care homes and childcare premises are required by law to undergo a criminal record check.

Basic Equipment Needed

There are number of reasons to have cleaning equipment, the most important of which should be making as great as possible cleaning routine. Other reasons for choosing a particular type of equipment include decreasing process of time, protecting the surroundings and the self or individuals.

(see the web wholesale section of this book for equipment sources.)

* **Carpet cleaning equipment**

* **Floor cleaning equipment**

* **Swimming pool cleaning equipment**

* **Cleaning windows equipmment**

* **Car Cleaning Equipment**

* **Air duct cleaning equipment**

CLEANING HOW TO DO IT....

1. Include step-by-step procedures for precleaning, cleaning during the job, and daily and final cleanings in project design or specifications.

2. Assign responsibilities to specific workers for cleaning and for maintaining cleaning equipment.

3. Have sufficient cleaning equipment and supplies *before* beginning work.

4. If contamination is extensive, conduct precleaning of the dwelling unit. Move or cover all furniture and other objects.

5. Conduct ongoing cleaning during the job, including regular removal of large and small debris and dust. Decontamination of all tools, equipment, and worker protection gear is required before it leaves containment areas. Electrical equipment should be wiped and high-efficiency particulate air (HEPA) vacuumed, not wetted down, to minimize electrocution hazards.

6. Schedule sufficient time (usually 30 minutes to an hour) for a complete daily cleaning, starting at the same time near the end of each workday after lead hazard control activity has ceased.

7. For final cleaning, wait at least 1 hour after active lead hazard control activity has ceased to let dust particles settle.

8. Use a vacuum cleaner equipped with a HEPA exhaust filter. HEPA vacuum all surfaces in the room (ceilings, walls, trim, and floors). Start with the ceiling and work down, moving toward the entry door. Completely clean each room before moving on.

9. Wash all surfaces with a lead-specific detergent, high-phosphate detergent, or other suitable cleaning agent to dislodge any ground-in contamination, then rinse. Change the cleaning solution after every room is cleaned.

10.	Repeat step 8. To meet clearance standards consistently, a HEPA vacuum, wet wash, and HEPA vacuum cycle is recommended. For interim control projects involving dust removal only, the final HEPA vacuuming step is usually not needed. Other cleaning methods are acceptable, as long as clearance criteria are met and workers are not overexposed.

11. After final cleaning, perform a visual examination to ensure that all surfaces requiring lead hazard control have been addressed and all visible dust and debris have been removed. Record findings and correct any incomplete work. This visual examination should be performed by the owner or an owner's representative who is independent of the lead hazard control contractor.

12. If other construction work will disturb the lead-based paint surfaces, it should be completed at this point. If those surfaces are disturbed, repeat the final cleaning step after the other construction work has been completed.

13. Paint or otherwise seal treated surfaces and interior floors.

14. Conduct a clearance examination.

15. If clearance is not achieved, repeat the final cleaning.

16. Continue clearance testing and repeated cleaning until the dwelling achieves compliance with all clearance standards. As an incentive to conduct ongoing cleaning and a thorough final cleaning, the cost of repeated cleaning after failing to achieve clearance should be borne by the contractor as a matter of the job specification,
not the owner.

17. Do not allow residents to enter the work area until cleaning is completed and clearance is established.

HUD COMMERCIAL CLEANING CHECKLIST

* Is the critical importance of cleaning in a hazard control project understood?

* Have all workers been trained and certified for hazard control work?

* Have the precleaning, daily, and final cleanings been scheduled properly and coordinated with the other participants in the hazard control process?

* Have cleaning equipment and materials been obtained?

* Do the workers know how to operate and maintain special cleaning equipment, and do they have directions for the proper use of all cleaning materials?

* Have all workers carefully studied the step-by-step procedures for precleaning (if needed), in-progress cleaning, and daily and final cleanings?

* Are all workers properly protected during the cleaning processes?

- Have provisions been made to properly contain and store potentially hazardous debris?

* Have dust-clearance testing and related visual inspections been arranged?

* Are the clearance criteria to be met fully understood?

* Have all appropriate surfaces been properly painted or otherwise sealed?

* Have appropriate records been maintained that document participants' roles in the hazard control project?

Equipment Needed for Cleaning

The following equipment is needed to conduct cleaning: high-efficiency particulate air (HEPA) vacuums and attachments
(crevice tools, beater bar for cleaning rugs), detergent, waterproof gloves, rags, sponges, mops, buckets,6-mil plastic bags,
debris containers, waste water containers,
 shovels, rakes, water-misting sprayers,
        and 6-mil polyethylene plastic sheeting.

HOW TO GET STARTED STEP BY STEP

Starting a business involves planning, making key financial decisions and completing a series of legal activities. These 12 easy steps can help you plan, prepare and manage your business.

Step 1: Write a Business Plan

Use these tools and resources to create a business plan. This written guide will help you map out how you will start and run your business successfully.

Step 2: Get Business Assistance and Training

Take advantage of free training and counseling services, from preparing a business plan and securing financing, to expanding or relocating a business from the Small Business Administration.

Step 3: Choose a Business Location

Get advice on how to select a customer-friendly location and comply with zoning laws.

Step 4: Finance Your Business

Find government backed loans, venture capital and research grants to help you get started.

Step 5: Determine the Legal Structure of Your Business
Decide which form of ownership is best for you: sole proprietorship, partnership, Limited Liability Company (LLC), corporation, S corporation, nonprofit or cooperative.

Step 6: Register a Business Name ("Doing Business As") Register your business name with your state government.

Step 7: Get a Tax Identification Number

Learn which tax identification number you'll need to obtain from the IRS and your state revenue agency.

Step 8: Register for State and Local Taxes

Register with your state to obtain a tax identification number, workers' compensation, unemployment and disability insurance.

Step 9: Obtain Business Licenses and Permits

Get a list of federal, state and local licenses and permits required for your business.

Step 10: Understand Employer Responsibilities

Learn the legal steps you need to take to hire employees.

Step 11: Get Equipment and Supplies

Get everything together that you'll need in order to actually operate. This includes items such as a truck, chemicals, equipment, and the various business forms such as service contracts. Once you have these things together, you can start the marketing process in order to get new customers.

Step 12: Your Marketing Plan

Coming up with your overall marketing plan, and implementing that plan. When you're just starting, it is usually best to choose one or two major marketing strategies, and work on those until you're getting a steady stream of customers. Once you've gotten good at once specific marketing avenue, then it's a good idea to move on to another one, and repeat the process. You can begin with "Zero cost marketing" and scale up once you are bringing in constant sales.

How to Write a Business Plan

Millions of people want to know what is the secret to making money. Most have come to the conclusion that it is to start a business. So how to start a business? The first thing you do to start is business is to create a business plan.

A business plan is a formal statement of a set of business goals, the reasons they are believed attainable, and the plan for reaching those goals. It may also contain background information about the organization or team attempting to reach those goals.

A professional business plan consists of ten parts.

1. Executive Summary

The executive summary is often considered the most important section of a business plan. This section briefly tells your reader where your company is, where you want to take it, and why your business idea will be successful. If you are seeking financing, the executive summary is also your first opportunity to grab a potential investor's interest.

2. Company Description

This section of your plan provides a high-level review of the different elements of your business. This is akin to an extended elevator pitch and can help readers and potential investors quickly understand the goal of your business and its unique proposition.

3. Market Analysis

The market analysis section of your plan should illustrate your industry and market knowledge as well as any of your research findings and conclusions. This section is usually presented after the company description.

4. Organization and Management

Organization and Management follows the Market Analysis. This section should include: your company's organizational structure, details about the ownership of your company, profiles of your management team, and the qualifications of your board of directors.

5. Service or Product Line

Once you've completed the Organizational and Management section of your plan, the next part of your plan is where you describe your service or product, emphasizing the benefits to potential and current customers. Focus on why your particular product will fill a need for your target customers.

6. Marketing and Sales

Once you've completed the Service or Product Line section of your plan, the next part of your plan should focus on your marketing and sales management strategy for your business.

7. Funding Request

If you are seeking funding for your business venture, use this section to outline your requirements.

8. Financial Projections

You should develop the Financial Projections section after you've analyzed the market and set clear objectives. That's when you can allocate resources efficiently. The following is a list of the critical financial statements to include in your business plan packet.

9. Marketing and Sales

Once you've completed the Service or Product Line section of your plan, the next part of your business plan should focus on your marketing and sales management strategy for your business.

10. Appendix

The Appendix should be provided to readers on an as-needed basis. In other words, it should not be included with the main body of your business plan. Your plan is your communication tool; as such, it will be seen by a lot of people. Some of the information in the business section you will not want everyone to see, but specific individuals (such as creditors) may want access to this information to make lending decisions. Therefore, it is important to have the appendix within easy reach.

How to make your business plan stand out.

One of the first steps to business planning is determining your target market and why they would want to buy from you.

For example, is the market you serve the best one for your product or service? Are the benefits of dealing with your business clear and are they aligned with customer needs? If you're unsure about the answers to any of these questions, take a step back and revisit the foundation of your business plan.

YOUR GOLDMINE OF GOVERNMENT GRANTS!

Government grants. Many people either don't believe government grants exsist or they don't think they would ever be able to get government grant money.

First lets make one thing clear. Government grant money is **YOUR MONEY**. Government money comes from taxes paid by residents of this country. Depending on what state you live in, you are paying taxes on almost everything....Property tax for your house. Property tax on your car. Taxes on the things you purchase in the mall, or at the gas station. Taxes on your gasoline, the food you buy etc.

So get yourself in the frame of mind that you are not a charity case or too proud to ask for help, because billionaire companies like GM, Big Banks and most of Corporate America is not hesitating to get their share of **YOUR MONEY**!

There are over two thousand three hundred (2,300) Federal Government Assistance Programs. Some are loans but many are formula grants and project grants. To see all of the programs available go to:

http://www.CFDA.gov

WRITING A GRANT PROPOSAL

The Basic Components of a Proposal

There are eight basic components to creating a solid proposal package:

(5)The proposal summary;

(6)   Introduction of organization;

(7)   The problem statement

(or needs assessment);

(8)   Project objectives;

(9)   Project methods or design;

(10)   Project evaluation;

(11)   Future funding; and

(12)   The project budget.

The following will provide an overview of these components.

1. The Proposal Summary: Outline of Project Goals

The proposal summary outlines the proposed project and should appear at the beginning of the proposal. It could be in the form of a cover letter or a separate page, but should definitely be brief -- no longer than two or three paragraphs. The summary would be most useful if it were prepared after the proposal has been developed in order to encompass all the key summary points necessary to communicate the objectives of the project. It is this document that becomes the cornerstone of your proposal, and the initial impression it gives will be critical to the success of your venture. In many cases, the summary will be the first part of the proposal package seen by agency officials and very possibly could be the only part of the package that is carefully reviewed before the decision is made to consider the project any further.

The applicant must select a fundable project which can be supported in view of the local need. Alternatives, in the absence of Federal support, should be pointed out. The influence of the project both during and after the project period should be explained. The consequences of the project as a result of funding should be highlighted.

2. Introduction: Presenting a Credible Applicant or Organization

The applicant should gather data about its organization from all available sources. Most proposals require a description of an applicant's organization to describe its past and present operations. Some features to consider are:

A brief biography of board members and key staff members.

The organization's goals, philosophy, track record with other grantors, and any success stories.

The data should be relevant to the goals of the Federal grantor agency and should establish the applicant's credibility.

3. The Problem Statement: Stating the Purpose at Hand

The problem statement (or needs assessment) is a key element of a proposal that makes a clear, concise, and well-supported statement of the problem to be addressed. The best way to collect information about the problem is to conduct and document both a formal and informal needs assessment for a program in the FF-4 11-08 target or service area. The information provided should be both factual and directly related to the problem addressed by the proposal. Areas to document are:

The purpose for developing the proposal.

The beneficiaries -- who are they and how will they benefit.

The social and economic costs to be affected.

The nature of the problem (provide as much hard evidence as possible).

How the applicant organization came to realize the problem exists, and what is currently being done about the problem.

The remaining alternatives available when funding has been exhausted. Explain what will happen to the project and the impending implications.

Most importantly, the specific manner through which problems might be solved. Review the resources needed, considering how they will be used and to what end.

There is a considerable body of literature on the exact assessment techniques to be used. Any local, regional, or State government planning office, or local university offering course work in planning and evaluation techniques should be able to provide excellent background references.

Types of data that may be collected include: historical, geographic, quantitative, factual, statistical, and philosophical information, as well as studies completed by colleges, and literature searches from public or university libraries.

Local colleges or universities which have a department or section related to the proposal topic may help determine if there is interest in developing a student or faculty project to conduct a needs assessment. It may be helpful to include examples of the findings for highlighting in the proposal.

4. Project Objectives: Goals and Desired Outcome

Program objectives refer to specific activities in a proposal. It is necessary to identify all objectives related to the goals to be reached, and the methods to be employed to achieve the stated objectives. Consider quantities or things measurable and refer to a problem statement and the outcome of proposed activities when developing a well-stated objective. The figures used should be verifiable. Remember, if the proposal is funded, the stated objectives will probably be used to evaluate program progress, so be realistic. There is literature available to help identify and write program objectives.

5. Program Methods and Program Design: A Plan of Action

The program design refers to how the project is expected to work and solve the stated problem. Sketch out the following:

The activities to occur along with the related resources and staff needed to operate the project(inputs).

A flow chart of the organizational features of the project. Describe how the parts interrelate, where personnel will be needed, and what they are expected to do. Identify the kinds of facilities, transportation, and support services required (throughputs).

Explain what will be achieved through 1 and 2 above (outputs); i.e., plan for measurable results. Project staff may be required to produce evidence of program performance through an examination of stated objectives during either a site visit by the Federal grantor agency and or grant reviews which may involve peer review committees.

It may be useful to devise a diagram of the program design. For example, draw a three column block. Each column is headed by one of the parts (inputs, throughputs and outputs), and on the left 11-08 FF-5 (next to the first column) specific program features should be identified (i.e., implementation, staffing, procurement, and systems development).

In the grid, specify something about the program design, for example, assume the first column is labeled inputs and the first row is labeled staff. On the grid one might specify under inputs five nurses to operate a child care unit. The throughput might be to maintain charts, counsel the children, and set up a daily routine; outputs might be to discharge 25 healthy children per week. This type of procedure will help to conceptualize both the scope and detail of the project.

Wherever possible, justify in the narrative the course of action taken. The most economical method should be used that does not compromise or sacrifice project quality. The financial expenses associated with performance of the project will later become points of negotiation with the Federal program staff. If everything is not carefully justified in writing in the proposal, after negotiation with the Federal grantor agencies, the approved project may resemble less of the original concept.

Carefully consider the pressures of the proposed implementation, that is, the time and money needed to acquire each part of the plan. A Program Evaluation and Review Technique (PERT) chart could be useful and supportive in justifying some proposals.

The remaining alternatives available when funding has been exhausted. Explain what will happen to the project and the impending implications.

Highlight the innovative features of the proposal which could be considered distinct from other proposals under consideration.

Whenever possible, use appendices to provide details, supplementary data, references, and information requiring in-depth analysis. These types of data, although supportive of the proposal, if included in the body of the design, could detract from its readability. Appendices provide the proposal reader with immediate access to details if and when clarification of an idea, sequence or conclusion is required. Time tables, work plans, schedules, activities, methodologies, legal papers, personal vitae, letters of support, and endorsements are examples of appendices.

6. Evaluation: Product and Process Analysis

The evaluation component is two-fold: (1) product evaluation; and (2) process evaluation. Product evaluation addresses results that can be attributed to the project, as well as the extent to which the project has satisfied its desired objectives. Process evaluation addresses how the project was conducted, in terms of consistency with the stated plan of action and the effectiveness of the various activities within the plan.

Most Federal agencies now require some form of program evaluation among grantees. The requirements of the proposed project should be explored carefully. Evaluations may be conducted by an internal staff member, an evaluation firm or both. The applicant should state the amount of time needed to evaluate, how the feedback will be distributed among the proposed staff, and a schedule for review and comment for this type of communication.

Evaluation designs may start at the beginning, middle or end of a project, but the applicant should specify a start-up time. It is practical to submit an evaluation design at the start of a project for two reasons:

Convincing evaluations require the collection of appropriate data before and during program operations;

If the evaluation design cannot be prepared at the outset then a critical review of the program design may be advisable.

Even if the evaluation design has to be revised as the project progresses, it is much easier and cheaper to modify a good design. If the problem is not well defined and carefully analyzed for cause and effect relationships then a good evaluation design may be difficult to achieve. Sometimes a pilot study is needed to begin the identification of facts and relationships. Often a thorough literature search may be sufficient.

Evaluation requires both coordination and agreement among program decision makers (if known). Above all, the Federal grantor agency's requirements should be highlighted in the evaluation design. Also, Federal grantor agencies may require specific evaluation techniques such as designated data formats (an existing FF-6 11-08 information collection system) or they may offer financial inducements for voluntary participation in a national evaluation study.

The applicant should ask specifically about these points. Also, consult the Criteria For Selecting Proposals section of the Catalog program description to determine the exact evaluation methods to be required for the program if funded.

7. Future Funding: Long-Term Project Planning

Describe a plan for continuation beyond the grant period, and/or the availability of other resources necessary to implement the grant. Discuss maintenance and future program funding if program is for construction activity. Account for other needed expenditures if program includes purchase of equipment.

8. The Proposal Budget: Planning the Budget

Funding levels in Federal assistance programs change yearly. It is useful to review the appropriations over the past several years to try to project future funding levels (see Financial Information section of the Catalog program description).

However, it is safer to never anticipate that the income from the grant will be the sole support for the project. This consideration should be given to the overall budget requirements, and in particular, to budget line items most subject to inflationary pressures. Restraint is important in determining inflationary cost projections (avoid padding budget line items), but attempt to anticipate possible future increases.

Some vulnerable budget areas are: utilities, rental of buildings and equipment, salary increases, food, telephones, insurance, and transportation. Budget adjustments are sometimes made after the grant award, but this can be a lengthy process. Be certain that implementation, continuation and phase-down costs can be met. Consider costs associated with leases, evaluation systems, hard/soft match requirements, audits, development, implementation and maintenance of information and accounting systems, and other long-term financial commitments.

A well-prepared budget justifies all expenses and is consistent with the proposal narrative. Some areas in need of an evaluation for consistency are:

> (13)the salaries in the proposal in relation to those of the applicant organization should be similar;

> (14) if new staff persons are being hired, additional space and equipment should be considered, as necessary;

(15) if the budget calls for an equipment purchase, it should be the type allowed by the grantor agency;

(16) if additional space is rented, the increase in insurance should be supported;

(17) if an indirect cost rate applies to the proposal, the division between direct and indirect costs should not be in conflict, and the aggregate budget totals should refer directly to the approved formula; and

(18) if matching costs are required, the contributions to the matching fund should be taken out of the budget unless otherwise specified in the application instructions.

It is very important to become familiar with Government-wide circular requirements. The Catalog identifies in the program description section

(as information is provided from the agencies)

the particular circulars applicable to a Federal program, and summarizes coordination of Executive Order 12372, "Intergovernmental Review of Programs" requirements in Appendix I. The applicant should thoroughly review the appropriate circulars since they are essential in determining items such as cost principles and conforming with Government guidelines for Federal domestic assistance.

General Small Business Loans:

Loan Program, SBA's most common loan program, includes financial help for businesses with special requirements.

Loan Program Eligibility

SBA provides loans to businesses; so the requirements of eligibility are based on specific aspects of the business and its principals. As such, the key factors of eligibility are based on what the business does to receive its income, the character of its ownership and where the business operates.

SBA generally does not specify what businesses are eligible. Rather, the agency outlines what businesses are not eligible. However, there are some universally applicable requirements. To be eligible for assistance, businesses must:

Operate for profit

Be small, as defined by SBA

Be engaged in, or propose to do business in, the United States or its possessions

Have reasonable invested equity

Use alternative financial resources, including personal assets, before seeking financial assistance

Be able to demonstrate a need for the loan proceeds

Use the funds for a sound business purpose

Not be delinquent on any existing debt obligations to the U.S. Government.

Ineligible Businesses

A business must be engaged in an activity SBA determines as acceptable for financial assistance from a federal provider. The following list of businesses types are not eligible for assistance because of the activities they conduct:

Financial businesses primarily engaged in the business of lending, such as banks, finance companies, payday lenders, some leasing companies and factors (pawn shops, although engaged in lending, may qualify in some circumstances)

Businesses owned by developers and landlords that do not actively use or occupy the assets acquired or improved with the loan proceeds (except when the property is leased to the business at zero profit for the property's owners)

Life insurance companies

Businesses located in a foreign country (businesses in the U.S. owned by aliens may qualify)

Businesses engaged in pyramid sale distribution plans, where a participant's primary incentive is based on the sales made by an ever-increasing number of participants.

Businesses deriving more than one-third of gross annual revenue from legal gambling activities

Businesses engaged in any illegal activity

Private clubs and businesses that limit the number of memberships for reasons other than capacity

Government-owned entities

Businesses principally engaged in teaching, instructing, counseling or indoctrinating religion or religious beliefs, whether in a religious or secular setting

Consumer and marketing cooperatives (producer cooperatives are eligible)

Loan packagers earning more than one third of their gross annual revenue from packaging SBA loans

Businesses in which the lender or CDC, or any of its associates owns an equity interest.

Businesses that present live performances of an indecent sexual nature or derive directly or indirectly more 2.5 percent of gross revenue through the sale of products or services, or the presentation of any depictions or displays, of an indecent sexual nature

Businesses primarily engaged in political or lobbying activities

Speculative businesses (such as oil exploration)

There are also eligibility factors for financial assistance based on the activities of the owners and the historical operation of the business. As such, the business cannot have been:

A business that caused the government to have incurred a loss related to a prior business debt

A business owned 20 percent or more by a person associated with a different business that caused the government to have incurred a loss related to a prior business debt

A business owned 20 percent or more by a person who is incarcerated, on probation, on parole, or has been indicted for a felony or a crime of moral depravity.

Special Considerations

Special considerations apply to some types of businesses and individuals, which include:

Franchises are eligible except when a franchiser retains power to control operations to such an extent as to equate to an employment contract; the franchisee must have the right to profit from efforts commensurate with ownership

Recreational facilities and clubs are eligible if the facilities are open to the general public, or in membership-only situations, membership is not selectively denied or restricted to any particular groups

Farms and agricultural businesses are eligible, but these applicants should first explore Farm Service Agency (FSA) programs, particularly if the applicant has a prior or existing relationship with FSA

Fishing vessels are eligible, but those seeking funds for the construction or reconditioning of vessels with a cargo capacity of five tons or more must first request financing from the National Marine Fisheries Service

Privately owned medical facilities including hospitals, clinics, emergency outpatient facilities, and medical and dental laboratories are eligible; recovery and nursing homes are also eligible, provided they are licensed by the appropriate government agency and they provide more than room and board.

An Eligible Passive Company (EPC) must use loan proceeds to acquire or lease, and/or improve or renovate, real or personal property that it leases to one or more operating companies and must not make any profit from conducting its activities.

Legal aliens are eligible; however, consideration is given to status (e.g., resident, lawful temporary resident) in determining the business' degree of risk

Probation or parole: Applications will not be accepted from firms in which a principal is currently incarcerated, on parole, on probation or is a defendant in a criminal proceeding

Loan Amounts, Fees & Interest Rates

The specific terms of SBA loans are negotiated between a borrower and an SBA-approved lender. In general, the following provisions apply to all SBA 7(a) loans.

Loan Amounts

7(a) loans have a maximum loan amount of $5 million. SBA does not set a minimum loan amount. The average 7(a) loan amount in fiscal year 2015 was $371,628.

Fees

Loans guaranteed by the SBA are assessed a guarantee fee. This fee is based on the loan's maturity and the dollar amount guaranteed, not the total loan amount.

The lender initially pays the guaranty fee and they have the option to pass that expense on to the borrower at closing. The funds to reimburse the lender can be included in the overall loan proceeds.

On loans under $150,000 made after October 1, 2013, the fees will be set at zero percent. On any loan greater than $150,000 with a maturity of one year or shorter, the fee is 0.25 percent of the guaranteed portion of the loan.

On loans with maturities of more than one year, the normal fee is 3 percent of the SBA-guaranteed portion on loans of $150,000 to $700,000, and 3.5 percent on loans of more than $700,000. There is also an additional fee of 0.25 percent on any guaranteed portion of more than $1 million.

Interest Rates

The actual interest rate for a 7(a) loan guaranteed by the SBA is negotiated between the applicant and lender and subject to the SBA maximums. Both fixed and variable interest rate structures are available.

The maximum rate is composed of two parts, a base rate and an allowable spread. There are three acceptable base rates (A prime rate published in a daily national newspaper*, London Interbank One Month Prime plus 3 percent and an SBA Peg Rate).

Lenders are allowed to add an additional spread to the base rate to arrive at the final rate. For loans with maturities of shorter than seven years, the maximum spread will be no more than 2.25 percent.

For loans with maturities of seven years or more, the maximum spread will be 2.75 percent. The spread on loans of less than $50,000 and loans processed through Express procedures have higher maximums.

All references to the prime rate refer to the base rate in effect on the first business day of the month the loan application is received by the SBA.

Percentage of Guarantee

SBA can guarantee as much as 85 percent on loans of up to $150,000 and 75 percent on loans of more than $150,000. SBA's maximum exposure amount is $3,750,000. Thus, if a business receives an SBA-guaranteed loan for $5 million, the maximum guarantee to the lender will be $3,750,000 or 75%. SBA Express loans have a maximum guarantee set at 50 percent. 7(a) Loan Application Checklist

The specific terms of SBA loans are negotiated between a borrower and an SBA-approved lender. In general, the following provisions apply to all SBA 7(a) loans.

Loan Processing Time

There are two 7(a) loan process options with different time frames. In addition to standard procedures, SBA Express processing offers an expedited turnaround.

Special Types of 7(a) Loans

SBA offers several special purpose 7(a) loans to aid businesses that have been impacted by NAFTA, provide financial assistance to Employee Stock Ownership Plans, and help implement pollution controls.

SBA Microloan Program

The Microloan program provides loans up to $50,000 to help small businesses and certain not-for-profit childcare centers start up and expand. The average microloan is about $13,000.

The U.S. Small Business Administration provides funds to specially designated intermediary lenders, which are nonprofit community-based organizations with experience in lending as well as management and technical assistance. These intermediaries administer the Microloan program for eligible borrowers.

Eligibility Requirements

Each intermediary lender has its own lending and credit requirements. Generally, intermediaries require some type of collateral as well as the personal guarantee of the business owner.

Use of Microloan Proceeds

Microloans can be used for:

Working capital,   Inventory or supplies

Furniture or fixtures,   Machinery or equipment

Proceeds from an SBA microloan cannot be used to pay existing debts or to purchase real estate.

Repayment Terms, Interest Rates, and Fees

Loan repayment terms vary according to several factors:

Loan amount

Planned use of funds

Requirements determined by the intermediary lender

Needs of the small business borrower

The maximum repayment term allowed for an SBA microloan is six years.

Interest rates vary, depending on the intermediary lender and costs to the intermediary from the U.S. Treasury. Generally, these rates will be between 8 and 13 percent.

Application Process

Microloans are available through certain nonprofit, community-based organizations that are experienced in lending and business management assistance. If you apply for SBA microloan financing, you may be required to fulfill training or planning requirements before your loan application is considered. This business training is designed to help you launch or expand your business.

Find a Microloan Provider

To apply for a Microloan, you must work with an SBA approved intermediary in your area. Approved intermediaries make all credit decisions on SBA microloans. For more information, you can contact your local SBA District Office.

Business Legal Structure

When you are starting a business, one of the first decisions you have to make is the type of business you want to create. A sole proprietorship? A corporation? A limited liability company? This decision is important, because the type of business you create determines the types of applications you’ll need to submit. You should also research liability implications for personal investments you make into your business, as well as the taxes you will need to pay. It’s important to understand each business type and select the one that is best suited for your situation and objectives. Keep in mind that you may need to contact several federal agencies, as well as your state business entity registration office.

Here is a list of the most common ways to structure a business.

An S corporation (sometimes referred to as an S Corp) is a special type of corporation created through an IRS tax election. An eligible domestic corporation can avoid double taxation (once to the corporation and again to the shareholders) by electing to be treated as an S corporation.

A partnership is a single business where two or more people share ownership.

Each partner contributes to all aspects of the business, including money, property, labor or skill. In return, each partner shares in the profits and losses of the business.

A limited liability company is a hybrid type of legal structure that provides the limited liability features of a corporation and the tax efficiencies and operational flexibility of a partnership.

The "owners" of an LLC are referred to as "members." Depending on the state, the members can consist of a single individual (one owner), two or more individuals, corporations or other LLCs.

Corporation (C Corporation)

A corporation (sometimes referred to as a C corporation) is an independent legal entity owned by shareholders. This means that the corporation itself, not the shareholders that own it, is held legally liable for the actions and debts the business incurs.

Corporations are more complex than other business structures because they tend to have costly administrative fees and complex tax and legal requirements. Because of these issues, corporations are generally suggested for established, larger companies with multiple employees.

A cooperative is a business or organization owned by and operated for the benefit of those using its services. Profits and earnings generated by the cooperative are distributed among the members, also known as user-owners.

Typically, an elected board of directors and officers run the cooperative while regular members have voting power to control the direction of the cooperative. Members can become part of the cooperative by purchasing shares, though the amount of shares they hold does not affect the weight of their vote.

Selecting The Right Business Name

Ask 500 people already in business how they decided upon their business name and you will get 500 different answers. Everyone has a story behind how they chose their own business name. Even if the business is named after their own birth name, there's a reason why this was done.

When you open a business, in a sense, you are causing a new birth to begin. This new birth was created from an idea alone by you or your associates. It will have its own bank account, it's own federal identification number, it's own credit accounts, it's own income and it's own bills. On paper, it is another individual! Just as if you were choosing a name for your own unborn child, you need to spend considerable time in deciding upon your business name.

There are several reasons why a good business name is vitally important to your business. The first obvious reason is because it is the initial identification to your customers. No one would want to do business with someone if they didn't have a company name yet.

This makes you look like an amateur who is very unreliable. Even if you call your company "Kevin's Lawn Service," a company name has been established and you are indeed a company. People will therefore feel more comfortable dealing with you.

Secondly, a business name normally is an indication as to the product or service you offer. "Mary's Typing Service," "Karate Club for Men," "Jim-Dandy Jack-of-all-Trades," "Laurie and Steve's Laundry," "Misty's Gift Boutique," and "Star 1 Publishers" are all examples of simple business names that immediately tell the customer what product you offer.

However, most people will choose the simple approach when naming their business. They use their name, their spouse's name, their children's names or a combination of these names when naming a business. The national hamburger-restaurant chain "Wendy's" was named after the owner's daughter.

However, research has proven that these "cutesy" names are not the best names to use for a business. Many experts claim that it makes the business look too "mom-and-pop-sie." However, this depends on the business. If you are selling something that demands this mood or theme to appeal to your market, it's best to use this approach.

Personally, I am inclined to name my businesses with catchy names that stick in people's heads after we have initially made contact. Names like, "Sensible Solutions," "Direct Defenders," "Moonlighters Ink," "Printer's Friend," "Strictly Class," "Collections and Treasures," and "Starlight on Twilight" are all good examples of catchy names. These types of names relate to your product or service but serve as a type of slogan for your business. This is a big help when marketing.

A friend I know owns a business called "Mint and Pepper." He grows and sells his own line of raw seasonings to people in the local area. At a get-together for small businesses, he passed out his business card. The card had a peppermint candy glued on the back and the slogan read: "Your business is worth a mint to us." This marketing concept not only got my friend noticed and remembered, but brought in several large orders for the business.

When you name a child, you may not decide upon a definite name until after they are born. You do this because a name is sometimes associated with a type of personality. When you name a business you may need to wait until you have a product or service to sell and then decide upon a business name before going into the business itself because your business name should give some clue as to what product or service you are selling.

A business named "Joe's Collections" normally wouldn't sell car parts and a business named "Charlie Horse" would not sell knitting supplies.

To generate ideas - begin looking at business signs everywhere you go. Notice which ones catch your eye and stick in your mind. Try and figure out "why" they stuck in your mind. Naturally, the business "Dominos Pizza" sticks in your mind because it is nationally known. These don't count!

Look around and notice the smaller businesses. Take your time. Within a few days you should be able to come up with a few potential business names.

Then, when you finally find a few names you really like - try reciting them to other people and get their opinion. It won't be long until your business will have the proper name that will carry it through it's life!

HINT:

Try to avoid very long names so they will fit into small display ads. Amalgamated International Enterprises can be easily presented as AIE - which is easier and shorter to spell.

Register Your Business Name

Naming your business is an important branding exercise, but if you choose to name your business as anything other than your own personal name then you'll need to register it with the appropriate authorities.

This process is known as registering your "Doing Business As" (DBA) name.

What is a "Doing Business As" Name?

A fictitious name (or assumed name, trade name or DBA name) is a business name that is different from your personal name, the names of your partners or the officially registered name of your LLC or corporation.

It's important to note that when you form a business, the legal name of the business defaults to the name of the person or entity that owns the business, unless you choose to rename it and register it as a DBA name.

For example, consider this scenario: John Smith sets up a painting business. Rather than operate under his own name, John instead chooses to name his business: "John Smith Painting". This name is considered an assumed name and John will need to register it with the appropriate local government agency. The legal name of your business is required on all government forms and applications, including your application for employer tax IDs, licenses and permits.

Do I Need a "Doing Business As" Name?

A DBA is needed in the following scenarios:

Sole Proprietors or Partnerships – If you wish to start a business under anything other than your real name, you'll need to register a DBA so that you can do business as another name.

Existing Corporations or LLCs – If your business is already set up and you want to do business under a name other than your existing corporation or LLC name, you will need to register a DBA.

Note: Not all states require the registering of fictitious business names or DBAs.

Registering your DBA is done either with your county clerk's office or with your state government, depending on where your business is located. There are a few states that do not require the registering of fictitious business names.

Business Tax Advantages

Every year, several thousand people develop an interest in "going into business." Many of these people have an idea, a product or a service they hope to promote into an income producing business
which they can operate from their homes.

If you are one of these people, here are some practical thoughts to consider before hanging out the "Open for Business" sign.

In areas zoned "Residential Only," your proposed business could be illegal. In many areas, zoning restrictions rule out home businesses involving the coming and going of many customers,clients or employees. Many businesses that sell or even store
anything for sale on the premises also fall into this category.

Be sure to check with your local zoning office to see how the ordinances in your particular area may affect your business plans. You may need a special permit to operate your business from your home; and you may find that making small changes in your plan will put you into the position of meeting zoning
standards.

Many communities grant home occupation permits for businesses involve typing, sewing, and teaching, but turn thumbs down on requests from photographers, interior decorators and home improvement businesses to be run from the home.

And often, even if you are permitted to use your home for a given business, there will be restrictions that you may need to take into consideration. By all means, work with your zoning people, and save yourself time, trouble and dollars.

One of the requirements imposed might be off street parking for your customers or patrons. And, signs are generally forbidden in residential districts. If you teach, there is almost always a limit on the number of students you may have at any one time.

Obtaining zoning approval for your business, then, could be as simple as filling out an application, or it could involve a public hearing. The important points the zoning officials will consider will center around how your business will affect the neighborhood. Will it increase the traffic noticeably on your street? Will there be a substantial increase in noise? And how will your neighbors feel about this business alongside their homes?

To repeat, check into the zoning restrictions, and then check again to determine if you will need a city license. If you're selling something, you may need a vendor's license, and be required to collect sales taxes on your transactions. The sale tax requirement would result in the need for careful record keeping.

Licensing can be an involved process, and depending upon the type of business, it could even involve the inspection of your home to determine if it meets with local health and building and fire codes. Should this be the case, you will need to bring your facilities up to the local standards. Usually this will involve some simple repairs or adjustments that you can either do personally, or hire out to a handyman at a nominal cost.

Still more items to consider: Will your homeowner's insurance cover the property and liability in your new business? This must definitely be resolved, so be sure to talk it over with your insurance agent.

Tax deductions, which were once one of the beauties of engaging in a home business, are not what they once were. To be eligible for business related deductions today, you must use that part of your home claimed EXCLUSIVELY AND REGULARLY as either the principal location of your business, or place reserved to meet patients, clients or customers.

An interesting case in point: if you use your den or a spare bedroom as the principal place of business, working there from 8:00 to 5:00 every day, but permit your children to watch TV in that room during evening hours, the IRS dictates that you cannot claim a deduction for that room as your office or place of business.

There are, however, a couple of exceptions to the "exclusive use" rule. One is the storage on inventory in your home, where your home is the location of your trade or business, and your trade or business is the selling of products at retail or wholesale.

According to the IRS, such storage space must be used on a REGULAR Basis, and be separately identifiable space.

Another exception applies to daycare services that are provided for children, the elderly, or physically or mentally handicapped. This exception applies only if the owner of the facility complies with the state laws for licensing.

To be eligible for business deductions, your business must be an activity undertaken with the intent of making profit. It's presumed you meet this requirement if your business makes a profit in any two years of a five-year period.

Once you are this far along, you can deduct business expenses such as supplies, subscriptions to professional journals, and an allowance for the business use of your car or truck. You can also claim deductions for home related business expenses such as utilities, and in some cases, even a new paint job for your home.

The IRS is going to treat the part of your home you use for business as though it were a separate piece of property. This means that you'll have to keep good records and take care not to mix business and personal matters. No specific method of record keeping is required, but your records must clearly justify and deductions you claim.

You can begin by calculating what percentage of the house is used for business, Either by number of rooms or by area in square footage. Thus, if you use one of the five rooms for your business, the business portion is 20 percent. If you run your business out of a room that's 10 by 12 feet, and the total area of your home is 1,200 square feet, the business space factor is 10 percent.

An extra computation is required if your business is a home day care center. This is one of the exempted activities in which the exclusive use rule doesn't apply. Check with your tax preparer and the IRS for an exact determination.

If you're a renter, you can deduct the part of your rent which is attributable to the business share of your house or apartment. Homeowners can take a deduction based on the depreciation of the business portion of their house.

There is a limit to the amount you can deduct. This is the amount equal to the gross income generated by the business, minus those home expenses you could deduct even if you weren't operating a business from your home. As an example, real estate taxes and mortgage interest are deductible regardless of any business Activity in your home, so you must subtract from your business Gross income the percentage that's allocable to the business portion of your home. You thus arrive at the maximum amount for home-related business deductions.

If you are self-employed, you claim your business deductions on SCHEDULE C, PROFIT(or LOSS) for BUSINESS OR PROFESSION. The IRS emphasizes that claiming business-at-home deductions does not automatically trigger an audit on your tax return.

Even so, it is always wise to keep meticulously within the proper guidelines, and of course keep detailed records if you claim business related expenses when you are working out of your home. You should discuss this aspect of your operation with your tax preparer or a person qualified in the field of small business tax requirements.

If your business earnings aren't subject to withholding tax, and your estimated federal taxes are $100 or more, you'll probably be filing a Declaration of Estimated Tax, Form 1040 ES.

To complete this form, you will have to estimate your income for the coming year and also make a computation of the income tax and self-employed tax you will owe.

The self-employment taxes pay for Social Security coverage. If you have a salaried job covered by Social Security, the self-employment tax applies only to that amount of your home business income that, when added to your salary, reaches the current ceiling. When you file your Form 1040-ES, which is due April 15, you must make the first of four equal installment payments on your estimated tax bill.

Another good way to trim taxes is by setting up a Keogh plan or an Individual Retirement Account. With either of these, you can shelter some of your home business income from taxes by investing it for your retirement.

HOW TO HIRE YOUR EMPLOYEE'S

If your business is booming, but you are struggling to keep up, perhaps it's time to hire some help.

The eight steps below can help you start the hiring process and ensure you are compliant with key federal and state regulations.

Step 1. Obtain an Employer Identification Number (EIN)

Before hiring your first employee, you need to get an employment identification number (EIN) from the U.S. Internal Revenue Service. The EIN is often referred to as an Employer Tax ID or as Form SS-4. The EIN is necessary for reporting taxes and other documents to the IRS. In addition, the EIN is necessary when reporting information about your employees to state agencies. Apply for EIN online or contact the IRS at 1-800-829-4933.

Step 2. Set up Records for Withholding Taxes

According to the IRS, you must keep records of employment taxes for at least four years. Keeping good records can also help you monitor the progress of your business, prepare financial statements, identify sources of receipts, keep track of deductible expenses, prepare your tax returns, and support items reported on tax returns.

Below are three types of withholding taxes you need for your business:

Federal Income Tax Withholding

Every employee must provide an employer with a signed withholding exemption certificate (Form W-4) on or before the date of employment. The employer must then submit Form W-4 to the IRS. For specific information, read the IRS' Employer's Tax Guide.

Federal Wage and Tax Statement

Every year, employers must report to the federal government wages paid and taxes withheld for each employee. This report is filed using Form W-2, wage and tax statement. Employers must complete a W-2 form for each employee who they pay a salary, wage or other compensation.

Employers must send Copy A of W-2 forms to the Social Security Administration by the last day of February to report wages and taxes of your employees for the previous calendar year. In addition, employers should send copies of W-2 forms to their employees by Jan. 31 of the year following the reporting period. Visit SSA.gov/employer for more information.

State Taxes

Depending on the state where your employees are located, you may be required to withhold state income taxes. Visit the state and local tax page for more information.

Step 3. Employee Eligibility Verification

Federal law requires employers to verify an employee's eligibility to work in the United States. Within three days of hire, employers must complete Form I-9, employment eligibility verification, which requires employers to examine documents to confirm the employee's citizenship or eligibility to work in the U.S. Employers can only request documentation specified on the I-9 form.

Employers do not need to submit the I-9 form with the federal government but are required to keep them on file for three years after the date of hire or one year after the date of the employee's termination, whichever is later.

Employers can use information taken from the Form I-9 to electronically verify the employment eligibility of newly hired employees by registering with E-Verify.

Visit the U.S. Immigration and Customs Enforcement agency's I-9 website to download the form and find more information.

Step 4. Register with Your State's New Hire Reporting Program

All employers are required to report newly hired and re-hired employees to a state directory within 20 days of their hire or rehire date.

Step 5. Obtain Workers' Compensation Insurance

All businesses with employees are required to carry workers' compensation insurance coverage through a commercial carrier, on a self-insured basis or through their state's Workers' Compensation Insurance program.

Step 6. Post Required Notices

Employers are required to display certain posters in the workplace that inform employees of their rights and employer responsibilities under labor laws. Visit the Workplace Posters page for specific federal and state posters you'll need for your business.

Step 7. File Your Taxes

Generally, employers who pay wages subject to income tax withholding, Social Security and Medicare taxes must file IRS Form 941, Employer's Quarterly Federal Tax Return. For more information, visit IRS.gov.

New and existing employers should consult the IRS Employer's Tax Guide to understand all their federal tax filing requirements.

Step 8. Get Organized and Keep Yourself Informed

Being a good employer doesn't stop with fulfilling your various tax and reporting obligations. Maintaining a healthy and fair workplace, providing benefits and keeping employees informed about your company's policies are key to your business' success. Here are some additional steps you should take after you've hired your first employee:

Set up Recordkeeping

In addition to requirements for keeping payroll records of your employees for tax purposes, certain federal employment laws also require you to keep records about your employees. The following sites provide more information about federal reporting requirements:

Tax Recordkeeping Guidance

Labor Recordkeeping Requirements

Occupational Safety and Health Act Compliance

Employment Law Guide (employee benefits chapter)

Apply Standards that Protect Employee Rights

Complying with standards for employee rights in regards to equal opportunity and fair labor standards is a requirement. Following statutes and regulations for minimum wage, overtime, and child labor will help you avoid error and a lawsuit. See the Department of Labor's Employment Law Guide for up-to-date information on these statutes and regulations.

Also, visit the Equal Employment Opportunity Commission and Fair Labor Standards Act.

Web Wholesale Resource Rolodex

As of the writting of this book all, of the companies below, website is up and have an active business. From time to time companies go out of business or change their web address. So, instead of just giving you just 1 source I give you plenty to choose from.

Carpet Cleaning

http://www.monsterjanitorial.com

http://www.chem-tex.com/

http://www.discount-carpet-cleaning-machines.com/

http://www.cws-direct.com/

http://goo.gl/A1vb5P

http://www.cleaning-equipment.com/

http://goo.gl/SSYpXk

www.carpetcentral.com

http://www.carpet-cleaning-equipment.net/

http://goo.gl/Eb90WL

Foreclosure cleaning network

http://www.foreclosurecleanupnetwork.com/

Cleaning supplies....

http://www.wholesalejanitorialsupply.com/

http://dollardays.com/wholesale-cleaning-supplies.html

http://www.janitorialsupplies4less.com/

http://www.cleanitsupply.com/

Air Duct Cleaning Equipment

1. http://www.rotobrush.com/air-duct-cleaning-equipment.aspx

2. http://www.extractionsystems.com/

3. http://www.air-care.com/products

4. http://www.ductcleanersupply.com/

5. http://www.nikro.com/air-duct-cleaning-equipment-supplies.aspx

6. http://www.hardware-wholesale.com/wholesale-duct-cleaning-equipment

7. http://www.cws-direct.com/SpinDuct-Professional-Air-Duct-Cleaning-Equipment-p/cws-spinduct.htm

8. http://www.alibaba.com/showroom/used-air-duct-cleaning-equipment-for-sale.html

9. http://www.hellotrade.com/atlantic-engineering-usa/air-duct-cleaning-equipment-featherlite.html

10. http://www.exportersindia.com/indian-manufacturers/duct-cleaning-equipment.htm

11. http://www.abatement.com/air-duct/air-duct-landing.htm

12. http://www.abatement.com/air-duct/start-up_a.htm

TRANSPORTATION

Used Trucks/CARS Online

http://gsaauctions.gov/gsaauctions/gsaauctions/

http://www.ebay.com/motors

http://www.uhaul.com/TruckSales/

http://www.usedtrucks.ryder.com/vehicle/Vehicle Search.aspx?VehicleTypeId=1&VehicleGroupId=3

http://www.penskeusedtrucks.com/truck-types/light-and-medium-duty/

Parts

http://www.truckchamp.com/

http://www.autopartswarehouse.com/

Bikes & Motorcycles

http://gsaauctions.gov/gsaauctions/aucindx/

http://www.bikesdirect.com/products/used-bikes/?gclid=CLCF0vaDm7kCFYtDMgodzW0AXQ

http://www.overstock.com/Sports-Toys/Cycling/450/cat.html

http://www.nashbar.com/bikes/TopCategories_10053_http://www.nashbar.com/bikes/TopCategories_10053_10052_-110052_-1

http://www.bti-usa.com/

http://evosales.com/

COMPUTERS/Office Equipment

http://www.wtsmedia.com/

http://www.laptopplaza.com/

http://www.outletpc.com/

Computer Tool Kits

http://www.dhgate.com/wholesale/computer+repair+tools.html

http://www.aliexpress.com/wholesale/wholesale-repair-computer-tool.html

http://wholesalecomputercables.com/Computer-Repair-Tool-Kit/M/B00006OXGZ.htm

http://www.tigerdirect.com/applications/category/category_tlc.asp?CatId=47&name=Computer%20Tools

Computer Parts

http://www.laptopuniverse.com/

http://www.sabcal.com/

other

http://www.nearbyexpress.com/

http://www.commercialbargains.co

http://www.getpaid2workfromhome.com

http://www.boyerblog.com/success-tools

American merchandise liquidators

http://www.amlinc.com/

the closeout club

http://www.thecloseoutclub.com/

RJ discount sales

http://www.rjsks.com/

St louis wholesale

http://www.stlouiswholesale.com/

Wholesale Electronics

http://www.weisd.com/

http://www.anawholesale.com/

office wholesale

http://www.1-computerdesks.com/

1aaa wholesale merchandise

http://www.1aaawholesalemerchandise.com/

big lots wholesale

http://www.biglotswholesale.com/

More Business Resources

1.   http://www.sba.gov/content/starting-green-business

home based businesses

2.   http://www.sba.gov/content/home-based-business

3.   online businesses

http://www.sba.gov/content/setting-online-business

4.   self employed and independent contractors

http://www.sba.gov/content/self-employed-independent-contractors

5.   minority owned businesses

http://www.sba.gov/content/minority-owned-businesses

6.   veteran owned businesses

http://www.sba.gov/content/veteran-service-disabled-veteran-owned

7.   woman owned businesses

http://www.sba.gov/content/women-owned-businesses

8.   people with disabilities

http://www.sba.gov/content/people-with-disabilities

9.   young entrepreneurs

http://www.sba.gov/content/young-entrepreneurs

ZERO COST MARKETING

The web-RESOURCE guide has plenty of web sites for you to find products at huge dicounts. Below are a few steps to market those products using
ZERO COST INTERNET MARKETING stratigies.

While there are many ways to market we are only going focuse on ZERO COST MARKETING. You are starting up. You can always go for the more expensive ways of marketing after your business is producing income.

FREE WEB HOSTING

Get a free web site. You can get a free web site at weebly.com or wix.com. Or just type "free web hosting" in a google, bing or yahoo search engine.

Free web hosting is something you can use for a varitey or reasons. However many free web hosting sites add an extention to the name of you web address that lets everyone know you are using their services. For this reason you eventually want to scale up once you start making income.

LOW COST PAID WEB HOSTING

Free is nice, but you when you need to expand your business it is best to go with a paid web hosting service. There are several that give you good value for under $10.00 a month.

1. Yahoo small business

2. Intuit.com

3. ipage.com

4. Hostgator.com

5. Godaddy.com

Yahoo small business allows for unlimited web pages and is probably the best overall value, but they require a years payment up front. Intuit allows for monthly payments.

For free ecommerce on your web site, open up a Paypal account and get the HTML code for payment buttons for free. Then put those buttons on your web site.

Step by Step basic zero cost web site traffic instructions

Step 1 zero cost internet marketing

Now that your web site is up and running you should register it with at least the top 3 search engines. 1. Google 2. Bing 3. Yahoo.

Step 2 zero cost internet marketing

Write and submit a press release. Google "free press release sites" for press release sites that will allow you to summit press releases for free. I you do not know how to write a press release go to www.fiverr.com and sub-contract the work out for only $5.00 !!!

Step 3 zero cost internet marketing

Write and submit articles to article marketing web sites like ezinearticles.com.

Step 4 zero cost internet marketing

Create and submit videos to video sharing sites like dailymotion.com or youtube.com. Make sure to include a hyperlink to your website in the description of your videos.

Step 5 zero cost internet marketing

Submit your web site to dmoz.org. This is a huge open directory that many smaller search engines go to get web sites for their database.

Getting Motivated to Start Your Business

The other day I was driving down a street in a commercial district and noticed a moving van. Two "blue collar workers" were busy loading office furniture in a company-owned vehicle. It was obvious that they were employees of this major company and I surmised they were making about $12 per hour.

I then thought about the normal lives these men probably lived. They had to punch a time-clock every day. If they were sick, they had to report to a boss and get permission to stay home. They had to depend on the company to pay them a weekly salary. They got paid the same amount of money every week and were lucky to get a raise every year or so.

Because of being controlled by a time clock at work, they naturally arranged their lives in the same fashion. They came home at the same time, ate dinner at the same time, looked forward to Friday for 2 days of rest but ended up cramming all their neglected responsibilities from the previous week into those 2 days.

The entire human race consists of two major groups of people: (1) Leaders and (2) Followers. Leaders have a built-in knack to not be happy with the normal flow of existence. Leaders are continually striving for a way out of this rat-race because they have a human characteristic of wanting to lead instead of follow.

But a good many of these leaders don't have a lot of money because they have been working for an employer all their lives. They recognize that they will never achieve the level of success they desire working for someone else. But they can't just leave their job and survive on their own. How could they pay the rent? Put their children through college? Buy the groceries? Pay Visa and Mastercard? With all these fears sitting in the leader will often exist as a follower because he or she doesn't believe they have a choice.

But they do! In fact, the answer is right under their noses. Allow me to explain . . .

Let's take the guy working for the moving company that I saw when I was driving down the street. He could offer the same service on weekends through word-of-mouth advertising. By placing a simple classified ad under Services Offered in the local newspaper, he could pick up a couple jobs a month and bring in an extra income.

Or how about the lady that just had a baby and wants to stay at home with it. Her maternity leave from her employer, only allows her 6 weeks. If she doesn't go back to work then she will either lose her job, her income or both. If her husband doesn't bring in enough money to support her and the baby she doesn't think she has a choice. The new mother will sacrifice money for her child.

But if this lady wants to stay at home with her child, why doesn't she start a home day-care center? That way, she would still make money and be able to be with her new child at the same time. Good for the child. Good for the mother.

Good for the family unit. Good for other working mothers who can trust a "mother-run" day care center versus a commercial one. Plus since the day care center is in this mother's home, she can charge 40% to 50% less than commercial day care centers and probably make more money compared to her old job.

Too often, people who want to break out of the mold and start their own business will seek for products and services they know absolutely nothing about. Someone told them they could make a lot of money doing this and doing that. But the truth is that it will take anyone longer to make money with a product or service that they have to learn. In fact, this learning period could take a year or more.

The person could easily be discouraged about a small business if it doesn't make any money by then.

So, if you are considering starting a small business; entertain the possibility of starting one based on the skills you already possess.

BONUS MATERIAL: CREDIT REPAIR

Credit can sometimes be the lifeblood of a business, but today many simply don't know their rights when it comes to credit.

The information below from the FTC (Federal Trade Commission) can help you to get a FREE CREDIT REPORT and begin to correct or remove any blemishes on your credit.

The Fair Credit Reporting Act (FCRA) requires each of the nationwide credit reporting companies — Equifax, Experian, and TransUnion — to provide you with a free copy of your credit report, at your request, once every 12 months. The FCRA promotes the accuracy and privacy of information in the files of the nation's credit reporting companies. The Federal Trade Commission (FTC), the nation's consumer protection agency, enforces the FCRA with respect to credit reporting companies.

A credit report includes information on where you live, how you pay your bills, and whether you've been sued or have filed for bankruptcy. Nationwide credit reporting companies sell the information in your report to creditors, insurers, employers, and other businesses that use it to evaluate your applications for credit, insurance, employment, or renting a home.

Here are the details about your rights under the FCRA, which established the free annual credit report program.

Q: How do I order my free report?

The three nationwide credit reporting companies have set up a central website, a toll-free telephone number, and a mailing address through which you can order your free annual report.

To order, visit annualcreditreport.com, call 1-877-322-8228. Or complete the   Annual Credit Report https://www.consumer.ftc.gov/articles/pdf-0093-annual-report-request-form.pdfRequest Form   and mail it to: Annual Credit Report Request Service, P.O. Box 105281, Atlanta, GA 30348-5281. Do not contact the three nationwide credit reporting companies individually. They are providing free annual credit reports only through annualcreditreport.com, 1-877-322-8228 or mailing to Annual Credit Report Request Service.

You may order your reports from each of the three nationwide credit reporting companies at the same time, or you can order your report from each of the companies one at a time. The law allows you to order one free copy of your report from each of the nationwide credit reporting companies every 12 months.

A Warning About "Imposter" Websites

Only one website is authorized to fill orders for the free annual credit report you are entitled to under law — annualcreditreport.com. Other websites that claim to offer "free credit reports," "free credit scores," or "free credit monitoring" are not part of the legally mandated free annual credit report program.

In some cases, the "free" product comes with strings attached. For example, some sites sign you up for a supposedly "free" service that converts to one you have to pay for after a trial period. If you don't cancel during the trial period, you may be unwittingly agreeing to let the company start charging fees to your credit card.

Some "imposter" sites use terms like "free report" in their names; others have URLs that purposely misspell annualcreditreport.com in the hope that you will mistype the name of the official site. Some of these "imposter" sites direct you to other sites that try to sell you something or collect your personal information.

Annualcreditreport.com and the nationwide credit reporting companies will not send you an email asking for your personal information. If you get an email, see a pop-up ad, or get a phone call from someone claiming to be from annualcreditreport.com or any of the three nationwide credit reporting companies, do not reply or click on any link in the message. It's probably a scam. Forward any such email to the FTC at spam@uce.gov.

Q: What information do I need to provide to get my free report?

A: You need to provide your name, address, Social Security number, and date of birth. If you have moved in the last two years, you may have to provide your previous address. To maintain the security of your file, each nationwide credit reporting company may ask you for some information that only you would know, like the amount of your monthly mortgage payment.

Each company may ask you for different information because the information each has in your file may come from different sources.

Q: Why do I want a copy of my credit report?

A: Your credit report has information that affects whether you can get a loan — and how much you will have to pay to borrow money. You want a copy of your credit report to:

☐ make sure the information is accurate, complete, and up-to-date before you apply for a loan for a major purchase like a house or car, buy insurance, or apply for a job.

☐ help guard against identity theft. That's when someone uses your personal information — like your name, your Social Security number, or your credit card number — to commit fraud. Identity thieves may use your information to open a new credit card account in your name. Then, when they don't pay the bills, the delinquent account is reported on your credit report. Inaccurate information like that could affect your ability to get credit, insurance, or even a job.

Q: How long does it take to get my report after I order it?

A: If you request your report online at annualcreditreport.com, you should be able to access it immediately. If you order your report by calling toll-free 1-877-322-8228, your report will be processed and mailed to you within 15 days. If you order your report by mail using the Annual Credit Report Request Form, your request will be processed and mailed to you within 15 days of receipt.

Whether you order your report online, by phone, or by mail, it may take longer to receive your report if the nationwide credit reporting company needs more information to verify your identity.

Q: Are there any other situations where I might be eligible for a free report?

A: Under federal law, you're entitled to a free report if a company takes adverse action against you, such as denying your application for credit, insurance, or employment, and you ask for your report within 60 days of receiving notice of the action. The notice will give you the name, address, and phone number of the credit reporting company.

You're also entitled to one free report a year if you're unemployed and plan to look for a job within 60 days; if you're on welfare; or if your report is inaccurate because of fraud, including identity theft. Otherwise, a credit reporting company may charge you a reasonable amount for another copy of your report within a 12-month period.

To buy a copy of your report, contact:

- ☐ Equifax: 1-800-685-1111; equifax.com
- ☐ Experian: 1-888-397-3742; experian.com
- ☐ TransUnion: 1-800-916-8800; transunion.com

Q: Should I order a report from each of the three nationwide credit reporting companies?

A: It's up to you. Because nationwide credit reporting companies get their information from different sources, the information in your report from one company may not reflect all, or the same, information in your reports from the other two companies. That's not to say that the information in any of your reports is necessarily inaccurate; it just may be different.

Q: Should I order my reports from all three of the nationwide credit reporting companies at the same time?

A: You may order one, two, or all three reports at the same time, or you may stagger your requests. It's your choice. Some financial advisors say staggering your requests during a 12-month period may be a good way to keep an eye on the accuracy and completeness of the information in your reports.

Q: What if I find errors — either inaccuracies or incomplete information — in my credit report?

A: Under the FCRA, both the credit report ing company and the information provider (that is, the person, company, or organization that provides information about you to a consumer reporting company) are responsible for correcting inaccurate or incomplete information in your report. To take full advantage of your rights under this law, contact the credit reporting company and the information provider.

1. Tell the credit reporting company, in writing, what information you think is inaccurate.

Credit reporting companies must investigate the items in question — usually within 30 days — unless they consider your dispute frivolous. They also must forward all the relevant data you provide about the inaccuracy to the organization that provided the information. After the information provider receives notice of a dispute from the credit reporting company, it must investigate, review the relevant information, and report the results back to the credit reporting company. If the information provider finds the disputed information is inaccurate, it must notify all three nationwide credit reporting companies so they can correct the information in your file.

When the investigation is complete, the credit reporting company must give you the written results and a free copy of your report if the dispute results in a change. (This free report does not count as your annual free report.) If an item is changed or deleted, the credit reporting company cannot put the disputed information back in your file unless the information provider verifies that it is accurate and complete. The credit reporting company also must send you written notice that includes the name, address, and phone number of the information provider.

2. Tell the creditor or other information provider in writing that you dispute an item. Many providers specify an address for disputes. If the provider reports the item to a credit reporting company, it must include a notice of your dispute. And if you are correct — that is, if the information is found to be inaccurate — the information provider may not report it again.

Q: What can I do if the credit reporting company or information provider won't correct the information I dispute?

A: If an investigation doesn't resolve your dispute with the credit reporting company, you can ask that a statement of the dispute be included in your file and in future reports. You also can ask the credit reporting company to provide your state ment to anyone who received a copy of your report in the recent past. You can expect to pay a fee for this service.

If you tell the information provider that you dispute an item, a notice of your dispute must be included any time the information provider reports the item to a credit reporting company.

Q: How long can a credit reporting company report negative information?

A: A credit reporting company can report most accurate negative information for seven years and bankruptcy information for 10 years. There is no time limit on reporting information about criminal convictions; information reported in response to your application for a job that pays more than $75,000 a year; and information reported because you've applied for more than $150,000 worth of credit or life insurance. Information about a lawsuit or an unpaid judgment against you can be reported for seven years or until the statute of limitations runs out, whichever is longer.

Q: Can anyone else get a copy of my credit report?

A: The FCRA specifies who can access your credit report. Creditors, insurers, employers, and other businesses that use the information in your report to evaluate your applications for credit, insurance, employment, or renting a home are among those that have a legal right to access your report.

Q: Can my employer get my credit report?

A: Your employer can get a copy of your credit report only if you agree. A credit reporting company may not provide information about you to your employer, or to a prospective employer, without your written consent.

For More Information

The FTC works for the consumer to prevent fraudulent, deceptive, and unfair business practices in the marketplace and to provide information to help consumers spot, stop, and avoid them. To file a complaint, visit ftc.gov/complaint or call 1-877-FTC-HELP (1-877-382-4357).

Get Our Video Training Program at:

(Zero Cost Internet Marketing complete 142 video series)

http://goo.gl/gQnSo4

Massive Money for Real Estate Investing

http://www.BrianSMahoney.com

Made in the USA
San Bernardino, CA
05 January 2020